SUPREME®
BAR REVIEW

Criminal Procedure

Bar Exam Review

Supreme Bar Review
30539 Pinetree Road, Suite 224
Cleveland, Ohio 44124

(866) BAR-PREP (toll-free)

SupremeBarReview.com

Printed in the United States of America.

ISBN-13: 978-1-936450-04-6

For information address:

Supreme Bar Review
30539 Pinetree Road, Suite 224
Cleveland, Ohio 44124

SupremeBarReview.com

TABLE OF CONTENTS

I. SEARCHES AND SEIZURES

AMENDMENT IV
The right of the people to be secure in their persons, houses, papers, and effects, against unreasonable searches and seizures, shall not be violated, and no Warrants shall issue, but upon probable cause, supported by Oath or affirmation, and particularly describing the place to be searched, and the persons or things to be seized.

A. INTRODUCTION

Fourth Amendment law is complicated by the fact that the Supreme Court has approached many questions under the "reasonableness" clause of the Amendment. Coupled with changes in the Court's composition over the years, this has produced fine distinctions in a number of areas and many, many rules and exceptions. Because the Court, on occasion at least, has propounded "bright line" rules for the benefit of police officers, many (though certainly not all) of the rules are fairly definite. There is no substitute for learning the rules, their nuances, and their exceptions.

In particular, you should focus on the different police actions, the required evidentiary basis for each, the scope and duration of the search or other intrusion, and whether a warrant is required or not. **Table I** in the **Appendix** to this chapter provides a brief summary of these factors for the major kinds of searches and seizures. It is important to understand the nature of the police action in an exam question, and then to be able to tell whether the required warrant and basis (if any) were present, and whether the scope or duration of the action were exceeded. Furthermore, facts discovered through one kind of police action can provide the basis to move to a more intrusive level. Evidence is often found through a chain of events. Each link must be analyzed for its conformance to the Fourth Amendment. One illegal link can taint the whole chain (see the section on **Exclusionary Rules**). Knowing the rules is essential for identifying these illegalities.

B. FOURTH AMENDMENT PROTECTION

1. **Searches defined.** A search is an invasion of a protected privacy interest. The Court has rejected the notion that privacy interests turn on common law property concepts. It has also rejected the idea that state law concepts define expectations of privacy.

   a. The Supreme Court has set out a two-pronged test to determine whether a privacy interest exists:

      1) First, there must be an expectation of privacy that society is prepared to regard as reasonable. This prong refers to objective reasonableness, and

      2) Second, there must be a subjective expectation of privacy on the part of the individual. In modern analysis, however, this step is virtually irrelevant.

Example: A retreats into a closed telephone booth and speaks in a quiet voice to B. A believes his conversation will remain private, and society regards this expectation as reasonable. Therefore electronic interception of A's conversation constitutes a search.

Example: If A possess illegal drugs in his home, but A leaves the window shade up so that the drugs are visible from the street, then the objective privacy accorded individuals for activity in their homes would be lost because A did not take adequate steps to ensure his privacy. To put it another way, even if A had a subjective intent to keep it private, this is not an expectation society would recognize as reasonable.

b. **Burden of proof.** The defendant bears the burden of proof to establish the objective reasonableness of his expectation.

2. **Protected Areas**

a. **House.** "House" is broadly construed to include virtually all structures that people commonly use as residences, whether on a temporary basis, such as a hotel room or on a long-term basis, such as an apartment. Houses also include buildings connected to a residence such as a garage. Offices, stores and other commercial buildings are included within the term.

b. **Curtilage.** Protection for the home extends to the **curtilage**, the area surrounding the home and associated with the "sanctity of a man's home and the privacies of life." A barn is not included in the curtilage, but a front porch or backyard area would be included within the curtilage. Factors:

1) proximity of the area to the home

2) is area included in enclosure surround home

3) the nature of the area's uses

4) steps taken to protect the area from observation

c. **Open fields.** Protection does **not** include open fields or vacant and undeveloped land outside the curtilage. For this reason, entry onto open field is not covered by the Fourth Amendment, and none of its requirements (e.g., probable cause, warrant) apply

3. **Papers.** "Papers" encompass personal items, such as letters, diaries and pictures, as well as impersonal business records.

4. **Effects.** "Effects" constitutes the residual component of the constitutional phrase "persons, houses, papers, and effects." For example, "effects" include

automobiles, luggage, and other containers, clothing, weapons, and even the fruits of a crime.

5. **Not a search.** Because a search is defined in terms of an invasion of privacy, and privacy is evaluated in terms of reasonable expectations, where such expectations cannot be sustained, there is no privacy and thus no search. A nonsearch is not regulated by the Fourth Amendment; it may be done for no reason or any reason at all. Here are some police actions that do not amount to searches:

   a. **Plain View**. What an officer may observe with her senses (or even certain technical enhancements) from a place she is entitled to be. In cases where a law enforcement officer has a right to be, the officer may seize evidence of incriminating character visible within her initial authorized presence. Plain view observations can be used as basis for a warrant.

   b. **Beepers and other enhanced technology.** If the enhanced technology merely increases the depth of information not otherwise protected by an expectation of privacy, the government's use of enhanced technology to see or hear better is not a search. However, if the enhanced technology provides information from areas which are protected by an expectation of privacy, then the enhancement invades privacy and constitutes a search.

      Example: The use of a hidden beeper to track a barrel of chloroform (used to manufacture speed) was not an invasion of privacy where the information gleaned consisted of movements over public highways. However, if the monitoring continued after the barrel was taken inside a house and was no longer visible from outside, then a beeper locating the barrel within the structure constitutes an invasion of privacy.

      Example: Training a thermal imaging device that reveals heat patterns within the home (indicative of marijuana grow lights), constitutes a search. The information obtained could not otherwise have been obtained without a physical intrusion– at least where, as here, the technology in question is not in general public use. ***Kyllo v. US*** (2001). This case will probably govern the use of all technological enhancements to the natural senses directed at a home.

   c. **Aerial surveillance.** No search occurs by visual surveillance from the air of a house or curtilage conducted in legal air space, since what a person knowingly exposes to the public is not subject to Fourth Amendment protection. Navigable airspace for fixed wing aircraft is above 1,000 feet; there is no minimum level for helicopters. So far, all aerial surveillance has been approved.

   d. **Canine sniffs.** Exposure of luggage, located in a public place or other place where the drug detection dog is authorized to be, to a "canine sniff" does **not** amount to a search because a "canine sniff" by a well-trained dog is 1) less intrusive than opening the luggage, and 2) the information obtained is limited to presence or absence of narcotics. While the Supreme Court has not directly addressed the question of sniffs of the person, it is likely they would be upheld on the same theory.

e. **Conversations.** An individual is held to assume the risk that anything said to another, or in their presence, may be revealed, recorded, or transmitted by their auditor. Any person may be surveilled in this way outside the Fourth Amendment. Thus, an informer, even one planted by the government, may reveal what she has heard the defendant say. She may also wear a wire or transmitter to record the conversation or broadcast it to another officer. No warrant or probable cause is required. If they are properly authenticated, tapes and listener testimony may be offered by the prosecution.

Watch Out!

This kind of monitoring requires that one of the participants consents to reveal the contents of the conversation. Electronic surveillance may **not** be used against persons who would otherwise have an expectation of privacy in their conversations without the consent of one of the participants.

f. **Garbage.** There is no Fourth Amendment search where the defendant exposes garbage in the public street for mixing with other trash before being carted away. There is no objective expectation of privacy in garbage because garbage left on street is readily accessible to animals, children, scavengers and snoops, and curb-side garbage is left to be conveyed by a third party.

g. **Pen registers.** Pen registers record the numbers dialed on a telephone by monitoring electrical impulses; they do not monitor the content of the conversations. Law enforcement use of pen registers is not a "search" within the meaning of the Fourth Amendment. Unlike wiretaps and bugs, which permit the police to acquire the contents of communications, pen registers only reveal the number called. The phone numbers of parties to a communication are necessarily made available to a third person, namely the telephone company, every time a call is made.

6. **Seizures of property.**
A seizure of property is an act that invades an individual's possessory interest in that property. Tangible property is seized in Fourth Amendment terms "when there is some meaningful interference with an individual's possessory interest" in that property. The general rule is that a "seizure" occurs when a police officer exercises control over defendant's property by destroying it, or by removing it from the suspect's actual or constructive possession. A house or office and its

contents are arguably "seized" when the police secure the premises. The fundamental predicate of a seizure is probable cause, the absence of which constitutes a Fourth Amendment violation.

A seizure of property does **not** occur under the following circumstances:

a. **Temporary possession.** No seizure occurs when an officer merely picks up an object to look at it or moves it a small distance, because any interference with a suspect's possessory interest in such circumstances is not "meaningful." Intimate looking could constitute a search, however.

b. **Beepers.** The addition of a hidden beeper does not meaningfully interfere with possession of a beeper-free barrel of chloroform. Hiding a beeper in the item is therefore not a seizure.

7. **Standing.** A defendant can complain about (or, has "standing" to raise) a Fourth Amendment violation only when that violation invades the defendant's own Fourth Amendment rights, as opposed to someone else's rights. A defendant's Fourth Amendment rights are violated only when the defendant has a legitimate expectation of privacy in the place being searched.

   a. **Own Person and Own Premises**. A defendant always has a legitimate expectation of privacy in her own person. Similarly, a defendant has a legitimate expectation of privacy in her own premises, even if she is not home at the time of the search.

   b. **Guests**. A temporary guest does not have a legitimate expectation of privacy merely because he is present at the house, unless he has some more significant connection. An overnight guest, for example, always has a legitimate expectation of privacy in the residence. In addition, a guest may have a legitimate expectation of privacy if he has a significant connection to the house, as shown by factors such as: (1) the length of the stay (more than a few hours); (2) previous significant connections with the resident; (3) using the house to store possessions with the owner's permission; or (4) engaging in non-commercial activities in the home.

   c. **Areas of the Premises**. A person may have a legitimate expectation of privacy only in certain areas of a house or building. A homeowner has a legitimate expectation of privacy in the entire home. A guest, however, may only have a legitimate expectation of privacy in certain areas: she would have a legitimate expectation of privacy in the guest room where she was staying, but not in the master bedroom where she had not been invited; she also has a legitimate expectation of privacy in common areas (such as a family room).

d. **Cars**.

i. **Owner**. An owner of a car has a legitimate expectation of privacy in the contents of that car, even if she temporarily loans it to another person. If the owner gives another person complete control over the car for an extended period of time, however, courts may hold the owner no longer as a legitimate expectation of privacy.

ii. **Possessor/Passenger**. A person in possession of a car, even if not the owner, has a legitimate expectation of privacy of the car if the owner is absent. If the car owner is present, however, a passenger is much less likely to have a legitimate expectation of privacy in the car.

iii. **Traffic Stop: Search of Car versus Seizure of Person**. As noted above, a passenger in car ordinarily does not have a legitimate expectation of privacy in the car. Thus, if a car is illegally stopped and then searched, the passenger lacks standing to contest the illegal search of the car. However, the passenger does have standing to contest the illegal traffic stop, because her person was seized by the stopping of the car.

e. **Ownership of Object Seized.** A defendant does not have a legitimate expectation of privacy simply because she owns the object seized. Instead, she must have a legitimate expectation of privacy in the place or thing searched (not just the object seized).

Example: Suppose police unconstitutionally search *A* with no probable cause or reasonable suspicion (and for no other proper reason), and find drugs. *A* claims the drugs belong to *B*. If the police try to prosecute *A*, *A* can successfully move to suppress the drugs as resulting from an unconstitutional search of her person. But if the police try to prosecute *B*, *B*'s motion to suppress will fail (even though the search of *A* was unconstitutional), because *B* has no legitimate expectation of privacy in *A*'s person. (*B* can of course defend on the ground that *A* is lying and the drugs do not belong to *B*.)

C. SEARCH AND ARREST WARRANTS

1. **Warrant searches.** The Fourth Amendment lays out certain requirements for search and arrest warrants, and the common law requires others, but the Amendment itself does not specify when warrants must be obtained for searches or arrest. As specified in this outline, many kinds of search and arrest practices have been found reasonable in the absence of a warrant and, sometimes, in the absence of probable cause as well. Nevertheless, a warrant is required for some searches, and certainly is a permissible basis for searches and arrests even where it is not required.

2. **Probable Cause.** The Fourth Amendment states that "Warrants shall not issue but upon probable cause." Probable cause is a measure of the probability that a crime was committed and (for searches) that evidence of it will be found. As a standard of proof, it strikes a balance between protection of individual liberty and the community interest in crime control.

   a. **Quantum of evidence needed to establish probable cause.** The Court has described probable cause as a "fair probability" that, in the case of searches, fruits, instrumentalities, or evidence of a crime will be found in the place to be searched. While probable cause is "not readily, or even usefully, reduced" to a mathematical formula, it is fair to infer that the probable cause standard does not demand that a belief in criminality be correct or even more probable than not.

   b. **Informants' tips.** In ***Illinois v. Gates***, the Court held that probable cause should be assessed under the "totality of the circumstances." Among the factors to be considered are:

      1) **Informant's veracity.** This can be established by a track record of accurate tips; some motivation to tell the truth; or corroboration of the tip.

      2) **Basis of knowledge.** This can be established by detail in the source of the information; corroboration, especially of non-public details of the tip can also help establish the informant's basis of knowledge.

      3) Strength in one factor can make up for weakness in another.

      4) The information is to be assessed by the standard of an experienced police officer.

   c. **Victim/witness statements.** May form the basis of probable cause even without a track record or corroboration of the reported information.

      Example: An individual reports to a police office that her purse was snatched and points to the perpetrator or gives a detailed description, which the arrestee matches. This constitutes probable cause to arrest despite the absence of a track record of reliability or corroboration.

   d. **Police observations.** Observations by the police, if they reach the threshold of a fair probability of crime, can form the basis for probable cause.

      Example: Police observe one individual hand another a small container, of the type often used to contain drugs, in exchange for cash. Probable cause exists to search or arrest for drug distribution/possession.

3. **Warrant application.** Warrants are issued by a judicial officer after an ex parte review of an affidavit which is supported by oath or affirmation.

   False information in affidavit. If the defendant makes a substantial preliminary showing that a false statement was made in the affidavit, he is entitled to a hearing on the issue. The remedy for such a faulty affidavit is to redact the affidavit of the erroneous facts, and to conduct the probable cause determination anew.

4. **Warrant contents.**

   a. **Prohibition against general warrants.** The Fourth Amendment text specifies that warrants shall particularly describe the place to be searched and the persons or things to be seized. Particularity limits the government to a search of no greater scope or intensity than is necessary to locate the items named in the warrant.

   b. **Particularity in describing persons.** Name and address of person to be arrested is sufficient particularity.

   c. **Particularity of place to be searched/and wiretaps.** The Court has been quite lenient in allowing law enforcement flexibility in describing the place to be searched, and especially so for wiretaps.

   d. **Particularity in describing the thing to be seized.** A warrant must describe the items to be seized with as much particularity as is reasonably possible. If the item is of a generic type (e.g., lumber) a general description will do.

5. **Magistrate neutrality**. The warrant issuing authority must be a judicial officer, but a clerk of municipal court may issue warrants for minor breaches of city ordinances. The Supreme Court has held that a magistrate lacked neutrality where he received $5 for each warrant issued and nothing for each denied.

   a. **Detachment.** The Court has held that a magistrate who personally visited a bookstore to determine which materials were pornographic lost the character of detachment.

6. **Standard of review of magistrate's probable cause determination.** A court reviewing the issuance of a warrant does not assess probable cause *de novo*, but instead looks to see if the issuing judicial officer had a "substantial basis" for her finding of probable cause.

7. **Magistrate error – Leon Exception.** The Court held in ***US v. Leon*** that a good faith exception to the exclusionary rule applies to a magistrate's errors in the determination of probable cause. In other word, if an officer relies in objective good faith on a warrant that – it is later found -- lacks probable cause, any resulting evidence will not be suppressed. "Objective good faith" means that a

reasonably well-trained officer would not have known the affidavit did not establish probable cause or was otherwise defective.

a. There can be no good faith reliance, however, where:

1) the affiant knew the affidavit was false;

2) the magistrate abandoned his role;

3) the affidavit was so lacking in indicia of probable cause as to render official belief in its existence entirely unreasonable; or

4) the scope of the warrant was exceeded.

b. **Unconstitutional Statute.** The Court has extended the "good faith" exception to warrantless searches and seizures made pursuant to a statute later declared unconstitutional.

c. **Court/police clerks.** The Court has extended the good faith exception to mistakes by court/police employees who mistakenly keypunched in data from police files to track arrestees.

d. **Other searches**: The good faith exception to the exclusionary rule does not apply.

8. **Informant identity.** In general, the defense does not have a right to discover the identity of confidential informants for purposes of a suppression hearing. If the informant has information relevant to **trial** issues, the prosecution may have to reveal the informant's identity.

9. **Warrant execution.**

a. **Exceeding the scope of the warrant.** Reasonable mistakes in executing the scope of the warrant do not make for an unreasonable search. The Court has also held that the discovery of post-issuance facts demonstrating that an otherwise valid warrant is unnecessarily broad (under the true facts) does not retroactively invalidate the warrant.

Example: Execution of a search warrant against the wrong apartment in a multi-apartment complex does not invalidate the search unless the mistake itself is unreasonable.

b. **Seizing items not specified in the warrant.** The plain view doctrine serves as an independent basis to seize clearly incriminating items not specified in the warrant whether or not the police had reason to know they were there.

Plain view seizures must pass a three-prong test, namely:

1) the officer is located in a public place or has authorization to be where he or she is at the time the evidence comes into view, e.g., warrant, consent, exigency etc.,

2) the police officer has a lawful right of access to the evidence in view, i.e., the access is consistent with his limited authorization, and

3) the officer has probable cause to believe the evidence is linked to a crime, the incriminating nature of the evidence being immediately apparent, i.e., without resort to further checking. Plain view seizures are permitted under the reasonableness clause of the Fourth Amendment.

   Example: A policeman who lawfully enters a house to check out the sound of gunfire cannot move stereo equipment to record its serial numbers. While the officer was entitled to be in the house without a warrant due to the exigent circumstances created by the gunshots, moving the stereo was a separate search that must be supported by probable cause. To put it another way, the serial numbers were not in plain view.

c. **Searching for items not described in the warrant.** Searching for items that could not otherwise be found while looking for the items described in the warrant is impermissible, as is searching persons not described in the warrant.

d. **Searching persons found on the premises where a warrant is executed.** A search warrant to search the premises implicitly authorizes temporary detention of occupants during search. Others found on the premises may be frisked for weapons if there is reasonable suspicion they are armed and dangerous, but a separate warrant is required to conduct a full-blown search of persons found on the premises.

   Example: While executing a Warrant to search the bartender and bar for cocaine, the police may frisk or pat-down bar patrons found on the premises if there is reasonable suspicion, but they cannot conduct a full-blown evidentiary search. However, if during the frisk or pat-down, the police detect contraband whose character is immediately apparent, the police may exceed the limits of the frisk and seize the illegal contraband under the plain feel doctrine.

e. **Knock and announce.** Police must ordinarily knock on the door of a dwelling and announce their presence before entering, forcefully or not. This common law knock-and-announce principle forms a part of the Fourth Amendment reasonableness inquiry. The Court has rejected categorical exceptions to the need for a knock and announce before entry. Instead, the police must have reasonable suspicion of resistance or destruction of evidence by those within before they may dispense with knocking and announcing.

Such a case-particular exception may be contained in the warrant or may arise at the time of its execution.

Note: The Supreme Court has ruled that a violation of the "knock and announce" rule would not result in suppression of the fruits of the resultant search — that is, that the exclusionary rule would not apply to searches that were illegal solely because of a violation of the knock and announce rule. Accordingly, the correct answer in a situation in which the police should have, but did not, knock and announce before entering a home is that the failure to knock and announce violated the 4th Amendment but the results of any search will nevertheless not be suppressed.

f. **Nighttime.** Federal Rules of Criminal Procedure 41(c) requires that "the warrant shall be served in the daytime, unless the issuing authority, by appropriate provision in the warrant, and for reasonable cause shown, authorizes its execution at times other than daytime."

10. **Exigent circumstances.** The police may enter a protected area without a warrant to search or arrest under exigent (emergency) circumstances. Probable cause to search or arrest is still required. The standard for determining whether a warrantless entry of a home is justified under the exigent-circumstances exception to the warrant requirement is whether the officers have probable cause to believe that if they do not enter immediately:

a. evidence may be destroyed or removed,

b. the suspect may escape,

c. harm will occur to the police or others, either inside or outside the dwelling; or,

d. they are in hot pursuit of a fleeing felon.

Example: If the police have reason to believe that an armed felon raced into a house, they may follow in pursuit without a warrant.

Watch Out!

The Court has disallowed use of the exigent circumstances exception to the warrant requirement where the crime is a minor misdemeanor.

Note: On the basis of exigent circumstances, the Court has upheld police stakeouts around or "campouts" on the premises while a warrant is being sought. It has also approved the exclusion of the occupant from the home for the same purpose.

11. **Consent.** The basic law of consent searches is that a validly obtained consent justifies an officer in conducting a search. Neither probable cause (nor any other level of suspicion) nor a warrant is required. Any evidence discovered may be seized pursuant to the plain view doctrine (discussed above).

    a. **Voluntariness.** A valid consent must be given voluntarily. "Voluntariness" is a question of fact to be determined from the totality of the circumstances of the individual case. To be voluntary, consent must be free from duress or coercion, express or implied.

    b. **Vitiating consent.** Factors supporting the conclusion that coercion impelled the consent include:

        1) a show of force by the police, such as a display of guns, that would suggest to the person that she is not free to refuse consent,

        2) evidence relating to the consenting person's age, level of education, emotional state, or mental condition that make it reasonable to infer that her will was overborne by the officer's conduct.

    c. **Absence of awareness of the right to refuse consent.** Police do not have to inform the person of the right to refuse consent. Consent is valid even though the suspect was not aware of the right to refuse.

    d. **Scope of a consent search.** A suspect may delimit the scope of consent and may withdraw consent. Objective parameters, not the unexpressed beliefs of the suspect, define the scope of the consent search. The standard is what would a reasonable person have understood the grant of consent to search to mean. Thus, consent to search a car for drugs includes all searchable areas where drugs could possibly be located, including containers in the car.

    e. **Third party consent to common areas.** Consent to search given by third parties may be upheld based on either of two theories:

        1) common authority over the premises: mutual use by persons having joint access or control for most purposes; or

        2) a reasonable belief by the officer that there was common authority even where the third party did not in fact have authority to authorize consent.

Watch Out!

The Supreme Court has ruled that an express refusal of consent by one party with joint authority over a home renders a warrantless search of the home unreasonable as to him regardless of whether another person with joint authority consented to the search.

D. PARTICULAR SEARCHES

The chart that appears in **Table I** of the appendix summarizes the most important aspects of different kinds of searches: whether or not a warrant is required; the necessary evidentiary basis for the search; the scope; the duration; and any other noteworthy aspects of the law of that search. This Table can be used as a quick summary of the most important features of common searches and seizures. It can also serve as a basis for evaluating the legality of the search. Once one knows the scope, one can then evaluate whether a warrant was required and whether or not the necessary evidentiary basis was present. Most of the table is self-explanatory, or is based on concepts already discussed. The following notes supplement Table I with explanations of particular searches this outline has not yet covered.

1. **Containers.** Containers are "effects" within the terms of the Fourth Amendment. Containers include suitcases, briefcases, backpacks, purses and any other item capable of containing another item. An individual ordinarily has an expectation of privacy in her containers. There are three ways in which a container may be searched:

   a. **Probable cause search.** With probable cause an officer may seize a container; it may not be opened, however, without a warrant. No warrant is required if the container is in a vehicle (below).

   Example: A drug dog "alerts" to a suitcase on an airport baggage carousel. This creates probable cause (see above) for the officer to seize the item and apply for a warrant to open it.

Watch Out!

Containers with no expectation of privacy. Certain containers are so indicative of illegal contents (e.g. crack vial), that their appearance alone provides probable cause to seize them.

   b. **Search incident to arrest.** Pursuant to a valid arrest the police may search containers within the area of the arrestee's immediate control (often called the

"***Chimel***" area). No additional basis for this search is required. **Note** the special rules on search incident to arrest in a vehicle (below).

c. **Inventory/booking search.** A person being booked into stationhouse or jail custody may be searched, along with items in his possession. Vehicle inventory search: see below.

2. **Automobile searches and searches of containers found therein.**

a. **Automobile searches based on probable cause.** With probable cause, automobiles and containers found therein may be searched without a warrant. In general, the scope of automobile searches extends to wherever probable cause exists to suspect that an item subject to seizure may be found.

Example: Police have probable cause to believe a van contains stolen TV's. They may search areas that might hold the TVs, including the trunk, but not the glove box or consoles.

Watch Out!

The "automobile exception" is an exception to the warrant requirement, not to the need for probable cause to search an automobile.

1) **Searches of automobiles away from the scene.** A warrantless search of an automobile that would be valid if it were conducted at the scene, i.e., at the place where it was stopped or first discovered, is also permitted if it takes place away from the scene.

2) **Containers.** A container that might contain the object of a search within a vehicle may be opened and searched without a warrant. This is true even if probable cause for the container existed before it was placed in the vehicle, and even if the container could not have been searched without a warrant before it was placed in the vehicle.

Example: Police have probable cause to believe drugs are in a vehicle. They may search anywhere in the vehicle drugs may be hidden, including the purse of a passenger.

Example: Police have probable cause to believe a particular suitcase contains contraband. They observe it being placed into the trunk of a car. They may search the trunk, seize the suitcase, and open it without a warrant.

b. **Search incident to arrest.** There are two exceptions to the warrant requirement that may apply when a person is arrested and taken into custody while driving her car.

1) **Interior of the car, when within reaching distance.** If the person arrested is unsecured and within reaching distance of the interior compartment of the car, the police may search the interior compartment (including containers therein, but not including the trunk) without a warrant. If, at the time of the search, the person arrested is no longer within reaching distance of the interior of the car, this exception does not apply.

2) **For evidence relating to the crime of arrest.** When the person is arrested and the police have "reason to believe [that] evidence relevant to the crime of arrest might be found in the vehicle," police may search anywhere in the car for which there is reasonable suspicion the evidence might be found.

Example: Police pull over a car for exceeding the speed limit. They arrest the driver when they discover she has a suspended license. Police also have reasonable suspicion, but not probable cause, to believe the driver is storing marijuana in the car. Police may ***not*** search for the marijuana under this exception, because the marijuana would not be evidence of the crime for which the driver was arrested – driving on a suspended license.

Watch Out!

Noncustodial citations. There is no lawful search incident to a traffic citation or any other form of noncustodial "arrest." However, there is no Fourth Amendment restriction on which offenses a state may designate for possible custodial arrest.

Watch Out!

Pretext Arrests. If authorized by law, an officer may use his or her discretion in taking a person into custody even if the arrest is a "pretext" to perform a search incident to the arrest.

c. **Inventory searches of vehicles.** Warrantless, suspicionless automobile-inventory searches are constitutional under the Fourth Amendment.

1) Automobile inventories respond to three distinct law enforcement needs:

a) to safeguard items in the car,

b) to present an accounting to rebut potential claims of theft, and

c) to confiscate any dangerous items left in the car.

2) **Scope and discretion in impoundment and inventory searches.** Police regulations must control generally the circumstances in which both impoundment and inventory are permitted. The inspecting officer may exercise discretion in impounding the automobile and in conducting the search as long as that discretion is exercised according to "standardized criteria." The Court has struck down inventory searches conducted without any criteria, for example, on when closed containers can be opened.

d. ***Terry* searches of automobiles.** The car interior, including containers, may be searched for weapons without a warrant on the basis of reasonable suspicion that an occupant is armed and dangerous. The plain view doctrine applies to items found in a car during a ***Terry*** search. In addition, passengers may be subjected to a ***Terry*** search if there is reasonable suspicion they are armed and dangerous.

e. **Consent.** The owner, driver, or one with apparent authority, may consent to a search of the car, and the scope of the consent is defined by the object being searched for. In stopping a car, any possible legitimate basis to sustain the stop controls the constitutional inquiry, not the subjective intent of the law enforcement officer. Once a car is stopped, the law enforcement officer may use the opportunity to obtain consent.

Note on pretext: In general, Fourth Amendment analysis concerns the objective circumstances. Searches and seizures that are sustainable under any legitimate basis will pass constitutional muster notwithstanding the subjective intent of the law enforcement officer. In other words, even if the stop or search was a "pretext" for criminal investigation, that motivation is irrelevant and does not render an otherwise lawful act unlawful.

3. **Administrative searches / special government needs searches.** Special government needs searches are based on the reasonableness clause of the Fourth Amendment and are evaluated by a balancing test, in which the individual's interest in liberty and society's interest in security are weighed against each other. Administrative (or special needs) searches are performed for a non-criminal

purpose, such as public health and safety, protection of the nation's borders, or maintenance of an educational environment. A search or seizure whose predominant purpose is enforcement of the criminal law does not qualify as an administrative search. Analysis of the justification of a special government needs search is made pursuant to the following balancing approach:

a. **Balancing test.** The Court has articulated a three-part test to make the categorical assessment of a "substantial interest, which would permit a suspicionless government invasion of privacy:"

    1) the gravity of the public concerns served by the search or seizure;

    2) the degree to which the search or seizure advances the public interest; and,

    3) the severity of the interference with individual liberty.

b. **Probable Cause and Warrants.** The result of this balancing is that probable cause of a specific offense is virtually never required, and a warrant is usually not required for an administrative search. The particulars vary for different kinds of administrative searches.

    1) Basis for search. In some instances the basis for the search can be general legislative standards, or all people who fall within a category of activity. In others, some degree of suspicion less than probable cause may be required.

    2) Except for health and safety inspections of homes and some businesses, a warrant is not required for administrative searches. Even there, an administrative inspection plan substitutes for probable cause.

c. **Particular Administrative searches.**

    1) **Homes.** May be inspected for health and safety violations with a warrant issued on the basis of reasonable legislative or administrative standards (e.g. age or type of building). Such a warrant is required.

    2) **Businesses.** Businesses ordinarily can be searched under the same conditions as a home. Businesses that are licensed or ones traditionally subject to governmental regulation, however, do **not** require a warrant for administrative searches.

    3) **Fire damaged structures.** A person maintains a reasonable expectation of privacy in his fire-damaged home, unless the fire is "so devastating" that no reasonable privacy interest remains in the ash and ruins. A fire-fighter may enter a structure to put out the fire and remain there "for a reasonable time" to investigate its cause without a warrant. The

warrantless entry is based on the fire exigency, and the stay is based on administrative duty to determine the cause of the fire. A re-entry of a home by a member of the fire department ordinarily requires a warrant. The nature of the warrant depends on the purpose of the re-entry. If the "primary object" is to gather evidence of criminal conduct, a traditional search warrant is required. If the purpose is to determine fire origin, an administrative search warrant suffices.

4) **Prisons.** No Fourth Amendment protections apply.

5) **Schools.** While the Fourth Amendment applies to school officials, they may search a student and her belongings on "reasonable grounds." This is less than probable cause and possibly less than reasonable suspicion.

6) **International checkpoints and border searches.** Persons may be stopped at the international border or its functional equivalent (*e.g.*, at an airport where an international flight arrives), and they and their effects may be searched, without a warrant and in the absence of any suspicion of wrongdoing, "pursuant to the long-standing right of the sovereign to protect itself from the entry of persons or objects dangerous to the nation." Such warrantless, suspicionless searches and seizures are "reasonable simply by virtue of occurring at the border."

   a) **Especially intrusive border searches.** If the officials have reasonable suspicion of criminal activity, the scope of a border search may exceed routine customs search,

      Example: A suspected drug trafficker may be detained until nature takes its course if there is reason to believe that she swallowed balloons containing drugs.

   b) **Roving border patrol.** Traditional Fourth Amendment standards apply to searches and seizures by roving border-patrol agents. Thus, absent reasonable suspicion of illegal presence in the country, agents may not detain a person in a vehicle even briefly for questioning, i.e., conduct a ***Terry***-level investigatory seizure. Nor may a vehicle be searched absent traditional probable-cause.

   c) **Fixed interior checkpoint.** In order to detect illegal aliens, vehicle occupants may be stopped at fixed checkpoints, and briefly detained to be questioned, without individualized suspicion of wrongdoing.

7) **Probationer/Parolee:** Where access by the probation or parole officer is a condition of supervision, a probationer's or parolee's residence or person may be searched on reasonable suspicion. No warrant is necessary.

8) **Checkpoints:** Checkpoints at which vehicles are stopped on a regular basis (e.g. every car, every other car) have been upheld when designed to assure road safety (alcohol) but not when the suspicionless seizure is aimed at regular law enforcement (drugs).

   a) **DWI Checkpoints:** The need to deter and detect drunk driving outweighs the minimal intrusion of a roadblock, and thus law enforcement officers may stop a driver without suspicion of wrongdoing and observe the driver's sobriety. The officer may then attempt to obtain consent to search. On the other hand, checkpoints stopping all drivers are unreasonable when employed for general crime detection, such as drug law enforcement.

9) **Suspicionless Drug Tests:** The Court has evaluated suspicionless drug tests by the government under the reasonableness clause of the Fourth Amendment, using its special needs approach. It has approved suspicionless urine testing of:

   a) Transportation workers involved in accidents;

   b) Law enforcement officers applying for jobs or promotions;

   c) Public school students participating in competitive extracurricular activities

   A ban on using the test results for criminal prosecution has helped sustain their legality.

   The Court has struck down suspicionless drug testing of candidates for public office and pregnant women for cocaine use when the results would be used to prosecute.

Watch Out!

Fourth Amendment *only* applies where the government conducts drug testing.

Private drug testing does **not** involve state action. Therefore, the Fourth Amendment would not apply.

4. **Electronic surveillance.** Electronic surveillance is regulated by Federal and State statutes, as well as by the Fourth Amendment. Title III of the Crime Control Act of 1968 as amended, includes the following:

   a) **Warrant.** A warrant (order) is required for nonconsensual electronic surveillance. To intercept wire or electronic conversations, the government must seek a warrant from a judge based upon probable cause. All such wiretaps have to be approved by senior Justice Department officials. The orders last for thirty days, but the government may seek renewal from the judge approving the warrant.

   b) **Coverage.** Title III covers wiretapping, interception of cell phone calls, email, and electronic or mechanical interception of oral conversations in which there is a reasonable expectation of privacy. This coverage includes private parties as well as state actors.

   c) **Consensual monitoring.** Title III allows one party to give permission to allow a phone conversation to be overheard or recorded without a court order. The government does not need to get a warrant to have an informant wear a wire or record a consensual conversation.

   d) **Sanctions.** Title III has a statutory exclusionary rule that is broader than the Fourth Amendment's, barring use in all judicial, administrative proceedings, including the grand jury. There are also civil and criminal sanctions for illegal surveillance.

E. SEIZURES

The Fourth Amendment expressly covers seizures, not only of real and other property, but of persons as well. For suppression purposes, the significance of a seizure of the person lies in its effect on any resulting discovery of evidence. **Table I** summarizes the law of seizures (see Appendix).

1. **Arrest**. The taking of a person into custody for the purpose of charging.

   a. **Probable cause** to believe that a crime has been committed and the suspect committed it is required for an arrest.

   b. **Arrest warrant**

      1) **Houses.** The Court has held that the Fourth Amendment prohibits warrantless, nonconsensual entry into a suspect's home to make a "routine" arrests, *i.e.*, absent exigent circumstances.

      2) **Public places.** The Court has validated warrantless arrests in public places except for misdemeanors not committed in the officer's presence.

c. **Search incident to arrest.** A search of the area within the suspect's immediate control incident to an arrest comes with the arrest. The Court has held that a full search of the person is permitted incident to a custodial arrest under the reasonableness clause of the Fourth Amendment. This same rule applies to arrests in vehicles. Thus, the police may search the entire passenger compartment, including containers, without a search warrant incident to a lawful custodial arrest of any occupant in the vehicle, so long as the person under arrest is within reaching distance of the interior compartment of the car.

d. **Protective sweep.** During a lawful entry to arrest, the arresting officers may

1) automatically, i.e., without probable cause or reasonable suspicion, conduct a "protective sweep" of the areas adjacent to the arrest for persons who might pose a danger to the officers or others, and

2) if there is reasonable suspicion that there are other persons who may pose a danger to the officers elsewhere, the officers may sweep the building to verify or dispel that suspicion.

e. Probable Cause Determination. When an arrest warrant has issued, a magistrate necessarily has reviewed the sufficiency of the underlying affidavit or criminal complaint. With warrantless arrests, before an extended restraint on liberty may be imposed there must be a probable cause determination by a judicial officer promptly after the arrest. This does not require an adversarial hearing, just a review of the complaint. If this review is combined with arraignment or first appearance, as it often is, it is presumptively reasonable if it occurs within 48 hours of arrest; detention beyond that time is presumptively unreasonable in the absence of extenuating circumstances such as emergency closure of the courts or mass arrests.

2. **Stops and frisks.** A ***Terry*** stop is a brief detention amounting to a seizure under the Fourth Amendment. It may be performed on the basis of "reasonable" or "articulable" suspicion. A limited search, a frisk outside of outer garments to feel for weapons, is permitted upon "reasonable suspicion" that the suspect is armed and dangerous.

a. **Reasonable suspicion** depends on the totality of the circumstances and requires articulable, objective facts, but gives credence to experience and police training. The Court has held that reasonable suspicion is a less demanding concept than probable cause both in the quantity and quality of the evidence. Thus, an anonymous tip predicting future public behavior that lacks the distinct corroboration for probable cause might suffice to provide reasonable suspicion. "Innocent" actions, in conjunction with circumstances, can establish reasonable suspicion.

Example: Drug-courier profile cases. An officer's observations may properly be supplemented by "consideration of the modes or patterns of operation of certain kinds of lawbreakers." The fact that a suspect's behavior and appearance conforms to a drug courier profile does not by itself constitute "reasonable suspicion," but it does have evidentiary significance. Thus, an airplane traveler may be briefly detained at an airport based upon reasonable suspicion where the traveler 1) traveled from a major source city; 2) paid for ticket in cash with a large sum of small bills; 3) traveled under an assumed name; 4) appeared to be nervous, and 5) made a quick trip a great distance.

Example: An anonymous tip describing an individual and reporting his possession of a weapon was insufficient to establish reasonable suspicion without some corroboration other than the person's presence at the location.

Example: Fleeing at the sight of police in a high crime neighborhood constitutes reasonable suspicion.

b. **Scope of a *Terry* stop.** A ***Terry*** stop is limited, both in time and degree of intrusiveness. Both must be reasonably related to the purpose of the stop: to confirm or dispel the suspicion. While the Court has upheld a detention of 20 minutes, it has disapproved one of 90 minutes. Movement of the suspect, especially to a more private, and therefore confining, location also tends to make the detention more like an arrest (requiring probable cause) and less like a stop.

Example: Moving the traveler to an office and holding his ticket for a lengthy period exceeded the limits of a ***Terry*** stop and constituted an arrest requiring probable cause.

c. **Scope of frisk.** A ***Terry*** frisk of outer garments is allowed when the officer has reasonable suspicion that the suspect is armed and dangerous. It is limited to a patdown feel for weapons and must stop when it is apparent there is no weapon. However, the officer may seize non-weapon contraband detected during a protective pat down search of the sort permitted by ***Terry***, so long as the search stayed within the bounds delineated by ***Terry*** and the officer knows it is contraband by plain view or feel. Plain feel seizures are evaluated under a three-prong test analogous to plain view seizures.

d. **Vehicles.** The Court has extended ***Terry*** to a weapons search of the passenger compartment of an automobile stopped during a lawful investigation of its driver. ***Mich v. Long*** authorizes a "frisk" of [portions of] an automobile for weapons if there is reasonable suspicion that the suspect has a weapon in the vehicle.

3. **Consensual encounters**

a. **Distinguished from a stop.** A "seizure" of a person occurs when a police officer's conduct would cause a reasonable person to believe that he is not free to terminate the encounter. If a reasonable person would feel free to go about his business in the circumstances, then the individual has not been seized. Instead, he is participating in a "consensual encounter." The officer need not inform the person that he may refuse to cooperate. The subjective impressions of the person accosted are irrelevant, as are the silent intentions of the law enforcement officer. The reasonable person in this test "presupposes an innocent person." A consensual encounter falls short of a seizure, and thus is subject to no Fourth Amendment restrictions.

b. **Consensual encounters.** During a consensual encounter the police may:

1) approach a person;

2) pose questions;

3) ask for identification or travel documents;

4) request consent to search.

Example: Accosting a suspect on a city bus and asking for permission to search his travel bag does not constitute a seizure because a reasonable person would know that he was free to decline the officer's request.

c. **Factors producing a seizure.** A police-citizen confrontation does not amount to a "seizure" unless the officer adds to the pressure inherent in the situation "by engaging in conduct significantly beyond that accepted in social intercourse." Such conduct includes:

1) pointing a police weapon;

2) encircling the suspect;

3) roughly touching the suspect; and,

4) speaking in a tone indicating commands rather than requests.

d. **Effectuation of a seizure.** A seizure occurs when the suspect submits to an assertion of authority [beyond the actions in (b) above]. Where the suspect flees rather than submits to police authority, seizure does not occur until the police officer lays on hands or applies physical force to restrain movement, even if ultimately unsuccessful.

Example: If after spotting a suspected drug trafficker, a law enforcement officer seeks to question the suspect but the suspect flees, the stop or arrest does not occur until the law enforcement officer has gained physical control over the suspect or applied force. Therefore, regardless of the justification for the seizure, the exclusionary rule does not apply to any contraband dropped by the fleeing suspect during the attempted escape because the tossing preceded the challenged seizure.

II. PRIVILEGE AGAINST SELF-INCRIMINATION

A. INTRODUCTION

1. Fifth Amendment:

   "No person…shall be compelled in any criminal case to be a witness against himself."

B. SCOPE

1. Allows witness to refuse to testify where a response might incriminate or lead to incriminating evidence, even if witness is innocent.

2. Applies to any investigative stage that calls for testimony that might incriminate in a later criminal proceeding; e.g. grand jury, civil discovery, administrative proceeding.

3. Fifth Amendment applies to possible incrimination under **state** or **federal** law – otherwise suspect could be whipsawed between the two.

4. Does not apply to questions the answer to which might incriminate under **foreign** law.

5. The compulsion referred to in the 5th Amendment is legal compulsion (contempt for refusal to answer) or the psychological or physical compulsion of custodial interrogation (see ***Miranda*** section below). Deprivation of prison "privileges" in response to silence does not rise to the level of compulsion.

6. Fifth Amendment protection is limited to testimonial evidence. Testimonial evidence is characterized by the disclosure of the contents of a suspect's mind and is generated when the suspect gives information. Demonstrating the quality of a voice, as in compelled recitation of words spoken by the perpetrator, is not testimonial. Nor is the compelled giving of blood, tissue, hair, handwriting, etc. samples.

7. Special effects of Fifth Amendment at criminal trial

   a. Defendant may not be called to stand by prosecutor (compare civil case), he need not take the stand and invoke the 5th Amendment.

   b. Prosecutor cannot comment on defendant's failure to testify at trial (compare civil).

   b. Statements made out of court may be used, if otherwise admissible – usually as a party admission.

C. IMMUNITY GRANTS

A grant of immunity substitutes for the self-incrimination privilege by giving protection against later prosecution stemming from the immunized statements. Immunity is granted by the judge based on a party (usually the prosecutor) application pursuant to statutory authority. A witness is not free to decline immunity. There are two kinds:

1. **Transactional immunity**
   Bars future prosecution, except for perjury, of immunized witness for any crimes mentioned in response to questions.

2. **Use plus derivative use immunity (often called "use immunity")**

   a. Neither the testimony itself nor any information directly or indirectly derived therefrom may be used against the witness, except in a perjury or false statement prosecution.

   b. If the witness is later prosecuted for the crime about which he testified:

      1) The court must hold a taint hearing;

      2) Prosecutors have the heavy burden of showing that they have legitimate independent source for the evidence, but

      3) Exploitation of immunized testimony in other, more indirect ways is often allowed; e.g., planning trial, cross-exam, interpreting evidence

      4) Immunized testimony cannot be used to impeach a witness who testifies at a later trial.

D. PRODUCTION OF DOCUMENTS

1. **Content.**

    a. Even where the contents of a document would incriminate the witness, there is no basis for invocation of the privilege on that ground because the papers were not created under any compulsion.

    b. Pursuant to a search warrant or a proper exception, law enforcement agents may search for and seize documents authored by a suspect without offending the Fifth Amendment.

2. **The act of production** of tangible items, including documents, in response to a subpoena may, however, have communicative aspects of its own. These include:

    a. acknowledgment of existence of the document or item

    b. acknowledgment of its possession or control

    c. authentication

    If production would tend to establish **any** of these, then the witness may refuse to produce on 5th Amendment grounds, unless these are a "foregone conclusion".

3. **Third party production.** To protect the attorney-client relationship if the papers are unobtainable by summons from client, they are unobtainable from attorney.

E. ENTITY EXCEPTION

Collective entity (corporation, union, etc.) has no 5th Amendment protection.

III. POLICE INTERROGATION

A. THREE CONSTITUTIONAL PROTECTIONS

1. Due process – Fifth and Fourteenth Amendments

2. Fifth Amendment Self-Incrimination Clause (***Miranda***)

3. Sixth Amendment Right to Counsel

B. DUE PROCESS

1. Bars involuntary confessions: coerced

    a. Improper police tactics

1) threats or physical harm

2) promises

Example: Withholding a medical treatment until a suspect provides an explanation for his injuries would constitute coercion.

2. Applies

a. even if confession is true

b. even if ***Miranda*** does not apply; voluntariness of the statements is not dependent on custody; applies even after ***Miranda*** rights have been waived

c. requires state action

d. voluntary does not mean of own free will; e.g., defendant who confesses after hearing "voice of God," has not given involuntary confession

C. *MIRANDA* DOCTRINE
(see Appendix, **Table II**)

1. From ***Miranda v. AZ***; reaffirmed in ***Dickerson v. U.S.*** (2000).

2. ***Miranda*** is based on the Fifth Amendment self-incrimination clause. Its reasoning is:

a. Fifth Amendment applies outside court; i.e., to interrogation when suspect is in custody or freedom of action otherwise curtailed

b. such custodial interrogation is inherently compelling of self-incriminating speech

c. warnings dispel this compulsion

3. **Therefore the four warnings are required.**

a. right to remain silent

b. anything said may used against suspect

c. right to presence of attorney (sometimes called 5th Amendment right to counsel)

d. right to free attorney if suspect cannot afford one

Note: The Court has allowed some deviation from the precise warnings it has prescribed: e.g., that an attorney will be appointed "if and when" suspect goes to court.

4. **Operation of *Miranda* where it applies.**

   a. if no warnings, the prosecution cannot use the statement in its case-in-chief

      1) even if suspect actually knew rights

      2) even if the statement was not incriminating when made

   b. an attorney need not be provided, but police must stop questioning if one is requested

   c. spontaneous statements are acceptable

   d. applies to all levels of crime, including misdemeanors

   e. applies to statements used at sentencing phase

5. **Custody.**

   a. ***Miranda*** applies only to custodial interrogation.

   b. Definition: in custody or otherwise deprived of freedom in a significant way

      1) Does not include when suspect is "focus" of investigation but is not otherwise in custody

      2) In home interrogation is generally not custodial.

      3) No custody even if suspect is in stationhouse if he is there voluntarily.

   c. A person can be seized for 4th Amendment purposes but not in custody for ***Miranda***;

      e.g.:

      1) Roadside stop; for example, traffic violation or DUI investigation

      2) Most ***Terry*** stops

6. **Interrogation.**

   a. **Definition:** express questioning or its functional equivalent: words or action that police should know are reasonably likely to elicit an incriminating response. In reaching this determination:

      1) police intent is relevant : if police intend to elicit an incriminating response it is likely to be interrogation

      2) known susceptibility of suspect is relevant

   b. Informers or undercover officers planted in jail: there is no compelling atmosphere; no interplay between interrogation and police custody. Therefore no ***Miranda*** warnings required (compare to 6th Amendment protections, below, which begin only after formal charge).

   c. **Exceptions:** No ***Miranda*** warnings required even though there is custodial interrogation:

      1) booking questions: administrative questions to secure biographical data necessary to complete booking or pretrial services.

      2) request to take breathalyzer

      3) public safety exception: questions reasonably prompted by concern for public safety. (e.g., discovery of a weapon or kidnap victim)

7. **Waiver of *Miranda* rights.**

   a. After the warnings, suspect may waive or invoke ***Miranda*** rights

   b. Waiver standard: waiver must be voluntary, knowing, and intelligent

      1) **voluntary** – product of free and deliberate choice; no intimidation, coercion, deception (as to rights, choices)

      2) **knowing and intelligent** – aware of rights and of consequences of abandoning them

      3) events occurring away from suspect irrelevant, including:

         a) the state of the evidence

         b) that an attorney was trying to reach suspect

      4) qualified waiver (e.g., no written statement) is still a valid waiver

8. **Waiver after invocation of *Miranda* rights.**

   a. **How invoked.**

      1) **Right to silence:** express invocation or refusal to talk

      2) **Right to counsel:** by an unambiguous request. Police have no obligation to stop questioning or clarify suspect's wishes after an ambiguous request for counsel (e.g., "Maybe I need a lawyer.").

   b. **Once rights invoked.** Permissible police response:

      1) **Right to silence:** ***Miranda*** is satisfied by "scrupulously honoring" the right to cut off questioning, but police may try to question again if there is a new charge, new questioner, and new warnings.

      2) **Right to counsel:** A request for counsel requires cessation of questioning until an attorney is provided and is present, unless the suspect voluntarily initiates a conversation with the police. The invocation continues even after the suspect consults with the lawyer: police still may not question him (unless the suspect initiates) unless the lawyer is present. However, police may try to question again 14 days after the suspect has been released from custody.

> ***Watch Out!***
>
> Invocation of the ***Miranda*** right to counsel bars not only further questioning on the subject of the interrogation, but also on any other crime, even by a different interrogator with new warnings (except after a 14-day break in custody)

D. SIXTH AMENDMENT RIGHT TO COUNSEL: *MASSIAH* DOCTRINE

(see Appendix, **Table III** for summary and comparison with ***Miranda*** doctrine)

1. **Based on Sixth Amendment right to counsel.** "In all criminal prosecutions the accused shall enjoy the right to . . . . . assistance of counsel."

2. **Protections begin:**

   a. **Once Sixth Amendment has "attached":** formal adversary proceedings have begun; e.g.,

1) arraignment

2) indictment

3) information

4) other formal charge

Note: An arrest or other form of custody does **not** by itself trigger 6th Amendment protections

> **Watch Out!**
>
> The suspect does **not** need to be in custody for 6th Amendment protections to apply.

b. **Invocation.** A defendant invokes his Sixth Amendment right to counsel, for purposes of interrogation, when a defendant unambiguously or unequivocally requests counsel upon being approached by the police for interrogation. A defendant cannot invoke his rights anticipatorily, such as announcing it at a preliminary hearing, but must invoke the right to counsel when approached for (or during) interrogation.

c. **Effect of invocation:** No deliberate elicitation of incriminating statements on that charge

1) by law enforcement agents, unless counsel is present or the suspect initiates conversation on the general subject and waives his rights, or

2) by undercover informants, including "jail plants," who engage the defendant in conversations about the charged crime. "Passive" listening by an informant is acceptable, however.

> **Watch Out!**
>
> In contrast to ***Miranda*** invocations, 6th Amendment rights are case-specific; invocation of the rights on one charge does not bar elicitation of statements on another, uncharged crime, even if the uncharged crime is factually related to the charged one.

Example: Defendant is arrested, arraigned, and released on bail. Police engage an informant who is wearing a recorder and send him to speak with defendant. He elicits incriminating statements about the charged crime and other crimes. Statements about the charged crime are suppressed; the others are not.

d. **Waiver.**

1) to known police officers: same conditions as a ***Miranda*** waiver

2) there can be no waiver to undercover informants

IV. THE EXCLUSIONARY RULES

A. STATE ACTION

Constitutional restrictions on criminal investigative techniques only apply to state actors, and not to private party searches, seizures, or interrogations. The principal inquiry in determining whether a private party's actions constitute "state action" is whether the party's action may be "fairly attributable to the state."

1. **Public functions.** The Supreme Court has found state action present when the government delegates to the private sector functions that are historically and traditionally governmental in nature.

   Example: If a municipality privately contracts out the operation of prisons, schools, and municipal parks, the employees of such private contractors would be considered state actors for Fourth Amendment purposes.

2. **Symbiotic relations.** The Supreme Court has held that a private party who is a "joint participant" with state actors acts under "color of state law." If the search has been requested or directed by a state actor, where the private party is participating jointly with state actors, or the state actor is present and tacitly approves the action, the Fourth Amendment will apply to the search.

   Example: Employees of a private mail carrier company partially open a package containing drugs and alert the police. As long as the police follow the private trespass without expanding the breach in any way, the invasion of privacy is attributable to the original private actors. However, if the police expanded the breach of private with a further invasion of privacy, the separate invasion by the police would constitute a violation of the Fourth Amendment.

B. PROCEEDINGS IN WHICH THE EXCLUSIONARY RULES APPLY

The exclusionary rules only apply in criminal trials and criminal forfeiture proceedings, and even then not for all purposes (see **Impeachment**, below). They do not apply at all in:

1. civil cases;

2. grand jury (except for Title III violations);

3. sentencing;

4. administrative proceedings: deportation, probation, or parole violation proceedings.

> **Watch Out!**
>
> A federal statute, 42 U.S.C. § 1983 provides compensatory relief in a separate civil trial against any person who under color of law violates the federal constitutional rights of any other person, but this statute has nothing to do with a criminal defendant's rights at trial.

C. FRUIT OF THE POISONOUS TREE

Application of the exclusionary rule requires there to be a causal connection between the violation and the discovery of the evidence. Evidence obtained in direct violation of a constitutional provision is generally excludable. In addition, evidence indirectly secured as a result of the original illegality is also excludable as a "fruit of the poisonous tree" subject to counter considerations of attenuation, inevitable discovery, or the independent source rule (below). Some particular examples and exceptions:

1. **Tangible Items.** Tangible items seized as a result of a Fourth Amendment violation will be suppressed. This applies to items seized as a result of a warrant issued on the basis of observations during an illegal search (except where there was reasonable reliance under ***Leon***, (above).

2. **Defendant's presence at trial.** The exclusionary rule does not apply to exclude the defendant's physical appearance at trial. In other words, the defendant cannot suppress himself. The Court's reasoning is that illegal police activity might have an evidentiary impact, but not a jurisdictional one.

3. **Confession as a fruit of illegal seizure.** Generally confessions following illegal seizures are suppressed even if ***Miranda*** warnings were given, unless there is a gap of longer than several hours between arrest and confession, or other intervening circumstances.

Watch Out!

Miranda warnings do not by themselves dissipate the taint of illegal arrest.

4. **Confession as fruit of illegal warrantless home entry to arrest.** If the only defect in the arrest is lack of the required warrant, statements taken in the home are suppressed. Statements taken outside the home are not.

5. **Witnesses.** The exclusionary rule generally does not apply to live witnesses as opposed to inanimate objects or statements. The witness' decision to testify is a matter of free will, which serves to break the causal link to the violation which produced the witness. A possible exception to this principle is where the illegal search or arrest is for the express purpose of discovering the identity of witnesses.

6. **Fruits of Miranda violations.** Given the long history of ***Miranda's*** treatment as a less than fully constitutional doctrine, the only suppressible fruits of ***Miranda*** violations are the statements themselves. Tangible items, witnesses, and subsequent statements (properly obtained) are not suppressed, even if the ***Miranda*** violation is the "but for" cause.

7. **Fruits of coerced confessions.** By contrast, fruits of coerced confessions, including tangible items, will be suppressed, as will fruits of testimony compelled under a grant of immunity.

D. LIMITATIONS ON THE EXCLUSIONARY RULE

1. **Independent source rule.** The independent source rule allows admission of evidence that was discovered by a means independent of the constitutional violation.

   Example: Police have probable cause to obtain a search warrant to search a house for stolen TV's. They break into the house and see the TV's. They then apply for a warrant, not mentioning their illegal entry or observations. As long as the entry did not motivate the warrant application, the pre-existing probable cause and the warrant constitute an independent source for the discovery of the TV's.

2. **Inevitable discovery rule.** When the evidence in question would inevitably have been discovered regardless of the police error or misconduct that actually led to the discovery, the evidence is admissible. Inevitable discovery infers a hypothetical independent source. The prosecution must prove by a preponderance of the evidence that the information ultimately would have been discovered by legal means. Although the fact that the legal route to the evidence was underway

at the time the evidence was found helps to establish inevitable discovery, this if not strictly necessary.

E. IMPEACHMENT

If the defendant takes the stand in his defense he may be impeached with illegally obtained evidence, in the form of prior statements or tangible items, that was inadmissible on the prosecution's case-in-chief. The prosecution may ask him about the evidence on cross-examination and/or may introduce it on rebuttal (subject to the Rules of Evidence). The Court has allowed this practice with respect to all Fourth, Fifth, and Sixth Amendment issues it has addressed, with the following exceptions:

1. **Witnesses for the defendant.** May not be impeached with evidence illegally seized from the defendant.

2. **Actually coerced statements.** Neither involuntary statements (see above) nor statements obtained under a grant of immunity (legal coercion) may be used to impeach.

   Example: The perpetrator of the crime had red hair. The defendant testifies at trial that at the time of the crime his hair was black. On rebuttal the prosecution can introduce recently purchased black hair coloring dye illegally seized from the defendant's home, for the purpose of impeaching defendant's testimony with the suggestion that he dyed his hair after the crime. The dye could not, however, be used to impeach a defense witness who testifies that defendant's hair was black on the day of the crime.

3. **Impeachment with silence.** The defendant's silence, when arguably he should have spoken, either prior to arrest or after it, may be used to impeach his testimony, subject, of course, to the rules of evidence. However, silence after ***Miranda*** warnings may not be used, nor may the suspect's invocation of ***Miranda*** rights.

F. STANDING

Standing concerns the issue of who may challenge a constitutional violation. The Supreme Court has reconfigured the issue of standing as a matter of personal expectations of privacy. Fourth Amendment rights are personal in nature and thus the operative question is not whether a violation has occurred somewhere, but whether the violation occurred to the person seeking to invoke the exclusionary rule. The usual question is whether or not the suspect herself had a reasonable expectation of privacy in the place searched.

1. **Examples:**

   a. **Home.** Those with a possessory interest in the home have an expectation of privacy there, including in phone conversations on their telephones to which they are not parties.

b. **Guest in home.** Overnight guests have standing; probably most social guests do; brief commercial visitors do not.

c. **Vehicles.** Owner and driver have standing; passengers do not have standing in areas such as glove box, under seats, trunk.

d. **Phone conversations**. Parties to phone conversation have standing to challenge the electronic surveillance

2. **Interest in item seized.** An interest in the seized item is not itself enough to confer standing, but is relevant to whether the defendant had an expectation of privacy in the place searched.

3. **Statements.** A defendant obviously has standing to object to the admission of his own statement. Hearsay rules usually exclude from trial out-of-court statements by others. However, should the issue of suppression challenges to another person's statement arise, the Court would likely follow 4th Amendment precedent and hold that a defendant has no right to suppress, for example, another person's coerced statement.

4. **Defendant's testimony.** If the defendant testifies at a suppression hearing to establish standing, such testimony cannot be used in the prosecution's case in chief. The Court has hinted that it could be used to impeach.

V. RIGHT TO COUNSEL

AMENDMENT VI
In all criminal prosecutions, the accused shall enjoy the right to be confronted with the witnesses against him; to have compulsory process for obtaining witnesses in his favor, and to have the Assistance of Counsel for his defense.

A. AVAILABILITY

1. **Right to retained counsel.**

   a. Defendant gets counsel of choice.

   b. Defendant can represent himself, so the right can be waived in court. Waiver requires the government to bear the burden of proof that the waiver is: 1) voluntary, 2) knowing, and 3) intelligent.

2. **Right to appointed counsel.**

   a. The Sixth Amendment right to free counsel for indigents was incorporated in 14th Amendment due process and made applicable to states by ***Gideon v. Wainwright*** (felony with incarceration)

b. Applies to:

1) Felony conviction, regardless of the punishment

2) Misdemeanors and petty offenses:

a) there is a right to counsel if any incarceration or suspended sentence of incarceration is imposed (***Argersinger & Scott***), no matter what level the charge

b) **actual** not authorized punishment controls

c) a defendant can be sentenced to non-incarceration punishment on a misdemeanor conviction without appointed counsel (e.g., fine)

3) Later enhancements based on legal uncounseled conviction are acceptable

c. Applies at all "critical" stages of a criminal case: e.g., preliminary hearing, live pre-trial ID after defendant is charged.

d. Denial of counsel right is never harmless error.

e. Defendant may waive this right, too.

3. Appointed counsel on appeal.

a. Appeal as of Right: There is a right to appointed counsel and to a free trial transcript if necessary for the appeal.

b. Discretionary Appeal: There is no right to appointed counsel on a discretionary appeal to a state supreme court or to the U.S. Supreme Court

B. EFFECTIVE ASSISTANCE OF COUNSEL

1. **Government interference with assistance of counsel.** Prejudice is presumed when the government interferes with the ability of the defense lawyer to carry out her adversarial duties. In such cases, a Sixth Amendment violation is established by demonstration of the state action, and there is no requirement to show prejudice or harm.

a. bar on attorney-client consultation during overnight recess for fear of coaching;

b. requirement that defendant be first witness;

c. bar on direct examination of defendant.

2. **Ineffective assistance of counsel claims.** A convicted defendant's claim that counsel's assistance was so defective as to require reversal of a conviction or death sentence has two components: error and prejudice.

   a. **Deficiency.** The defendant must show that counsel's performance was deficient. Error is established where the defendant shows that counsel's representation fell below an objective standard of reasonableness. The proper measure of attorney performance remains simply reasonableness under prevailing professional norms. In this regard, the ABA Standards for Criminal Justice are a guide, and do not impose mandatory requirements of representation.

   Example: defense counsel relying solely on police reports without independent investigation is ineffective assistance.

   Example: ignorance of the substantive law governing the crime is ineffective assistance.

   b. **Not *per se* deficiency.** Truncated preparation time or lack of experience or expertise alone do not establish an ineffective assistance of counsel claim.

      1) **Federal forfeiture law** permitting confiscation of drug proceeds in advance of trial was not a denial of Sixth Amendment right to counsel as the right to retain a counsel of one's own choosing does not go beyond the "individual's right to spend his own money" to obtain the advice and assistance of counsel.

      2) **Lack of rapport.** There is no Sixth Amendment violation where defendant claimed a last minute substitution denied defendant a "meaningful attorney-client relationship." Rapport is not inherent in the Sixth Amendment guarantee of a right to effective assistance of counsel.

      3) **Strategic choices:** There is a presumption of high deference to strategic choices by counsel. Thus, questionable defense decisions concerning investigation, objections, testimony, *etc*., which can be explained by reference to trial strategy are not errors.

   c. **Prejudice prong.** The defendant must show that the deficient performance actually prejudiced the defense. Defendant must show that counsel's unprofessional errors raise a "reasonable probability" of a different outcome.

   Example: sleeping by counsel during trial is sometimes ineffective assistance.

   Example: joint representation of two or more accuseds who have an actual conflict of interest is *per se* prejudicial.

VI. PRE-TRIAL IDENTIFICATION

A. INTRODUCTION

1. **Terms**
   a. line-up – live viewing of suspect and others
   b. photo spread/array – display of photos of suspect and others (photo lineup)
   c. show-up – presentation of suspect **alone** to witness

2. These are forms of **out**-of-court ID. They can be testified to **in** court (at trial).

   a. **Non-hearsay:** even though the witness is testifying to his own out-of-court statement, for its truth, it is defined out of hearsay by FRE 801(d)(1)(C) – statement of prior identification by a witness now testifying and subject to cross examination

   b. **In-court identification:** Identification of defendant as the perpetrator at trial

3. Pre-trial identification techniques may raise three constitutional questions:

   a. **Detention of suspect** – Fourth Amendment

   b. **Right to counsel** – Sixth Amendment

   c. **Fundamental Fairness** – Fifth Amendment and Fourteenth Amendment Due Process

B. DETENTION

1. Keep in mind that the suspect must be lawfully in custody, or the out-of-court identification may be suppressed as a poisoned fruit of an illegal seizure.

2. If there is probable cause to arrest suspect – detention OK

3. If suspect is in custody on other charge – usually OK

4. If suspect not yet in custody, usually reasonable suspicion or a grand jury subpoena is necessary to compel appearance.

C. RIGHT TO COUNSEL

1. ***Wade-Gilbert*** **-** established a right to counsel at a lineup in order to protect defendant's right to cross-examine at trial. The theory is that there is a grave risk of prejudice at the lineup, which cannot adequately be reconstructed at trial through witness testimony, including that of the defendant. To prevent prejudice and/or reconstruct the ID procedure, the Court created a Sixth Amendment right to counsel at the ID stage.

2. ***Kirby v. Illinois*** – court limited the right to counsel at pre-trial ID to those conducted after the Sixth Amendment right to counsel "attaches". This seriously cut back sphere of ***Wade-Gilbert*** right.

   Note: It therefore is important to check the timing of the pretrial ID procedure. If it occurred **before** formal adversary proceedings began (see above) there is no right to counsel. There is, however, a due process right.

3. ***Ash*** – Defendant's Sixth Amendment rights had attached (indictment) when prosecutor showed witnesses photo array, but this was not the kind of live confrontation that made the procedure a "critical stage" of the prosecution.

4. **Summary:** The right to counsel only applies to live display (lineup, show-up) of a suspect after formal adversary proceedings have begun.

D. DUE PROCESS

1. **Theory:** unnecessary suggestion in ID procedure is conducive to mistaken ID at trial, which denies fundamental fairness. Elements of a due process claim:

   a. **Suggestive** procedure

      1) Show-up – *per se* suggestive

      2) Lineup composition or police communication can make the procedure suggestive

   b. **Unnecessarily** suggestive

   > **Watch Out!**
   >
   > A suggestive ID can be necessary, when, for example the witness may be dying.

   c. **Unreliability**. Was it nevertheless reliable, even if unnecessarily suggestive? Balance the effect of suggestion against factors concerning reliability, such as:

      1) Opportunity to view

      2) Witness' degree of attention

      3) Accuracy of prior description by witness

4) Witness' level of certainty

5) The time lapse between the crime and the ID procedure

Only unreliable identifications are suppressed.

2. **Suppression.** If (a) and (b) present, and under (c) the resulting identification was unreliable, the out-of-court ID is suppressed. If such a tainted out-of-court ID has a lasting effect, suppress in-court ID as well.

3. **Conduct of suppression hearing and trial.**

   a. Hearing (often called ***Stovall*** hearing) may be combined with trial.

   b. If defendant loses suppression hearing, at trial he may still attempt to attack conduct of out-of-court identification procedure in order to diminish its credibility or subsequent in-court identification with the jury.

4. **Scope.** Due process challenge may be raised against **any** identification procedure, regardless of whether adversary proceedings have begun or not.

VII. DOUBLE JEOPARDY

A. INTRODUCTION

1. **Constitution: Fifth Amendment**

   No person shall "be subject for the same offense to be twice put in jeopardy of life or limb."

2. **Rationale for the double jeopardy provision.**

   a. Finality.

   b. Repeated attempts at conviction unacceptably increase the risk that an innocent person will be found guilty.

   c. Fairness to defendants demands that the government limit itself to one effort to establish defendant's guilt.

   d. Nullification. A second trial could nullify the findings of the first.

3. **Multiple prosecutions for the "same offense."**

   a. Double jeopardy bars successive prosecutions by the same sovereign, whether after conviction or acquittal, for the "same offense."

b. Definition of same offense: the two offenses have identical statutory elements or one is a lesser included offense of the other. On the other hand, if each provision requires proof of a fact the other does not, they are separate offenses (***Blockburger v. U.S.***).

Example: A conviction for burglary and a conviction for breaking and entering based on the same event may not stand because breaking and entering does not contain an element that the burglary does not.

4. **Jeopardy.**
Jeopardy attaches (a) when jury is sworn, or (b) in a bench trial when the first witness is sworn, or (c) when defendant pleads guilty and the court accepts the plea and enters judgment of conviction.

5. **Scope.**
The double jeopardy clause generally does not apply to civil or administrative penalties or criminal forfeitures arising from the same event as a criminal prosecution.

a. **Contempts.** Conviction for a criminal contempt (a contempt designed to punish rather than to bring about compliance with the law) bars subsequent conviction for the same misconduct.

b. **Administrative proceedings.** The mere legislative or executive designation of a proceeding as administrative is not dispositive of the proceeding's true character. A court must evaluate the administrative proceeding to determine whether it is punitive in nature. The factors the court will look at are:

1) whether the sanction involves an affirmative disability or restraint;

2) whether it has historically been regarded as a punishment;

3) whether it comes into play only on a finding of scienter;

4) whether its operation will promote the traditional aims of punishment — retribution and deterrence;

5) whether the behavior to which it applies is already a crime;

6) whether an alternative purpose to which it may rationally be connected is assignable for it; and

7) whether it appears excessive in relation to the alternative purpose assigned.

Summary: Only the strongest balance of a totality of the aforementioned factors will permit a court to designate the administrative proceeding as punitive in nature and thus implicate the double jeopardy clause.

Example: A driver is arrested for drunk driving after blowing a .12 alcohol content on a Breathalyzer. His license is administratively suspended for one year. He is then prosecuted for driving while intoxicated. No double jeopardy violation.

c. **Civil forfeitures.** In rem civil forfeitures are neither "punishment" nor criminal for purposes of the Double Jeopardy Clause.

d. **Involuntary confinement.** Involuntary confinement following criminal incarceration is not double jeopardy. The involuntary confinement is not multiple punishment for the same misconduct because the involuntary confinement is civil, and not punishment.

6. **Dual sovereigns doctrine.**
Successive prosecutions based on the same conduct are permissible if they are brought by separate and distinct "sovereigns." On the theory that the states and the federal government are separate sovereigns, each may prosecute for the same conduct; the separate prosecutions are considered prosecutions for different "offenses" and are not barred by the double jeopardy clause. Whether the first prosecution resulted in acquittal or conviction is of no consequence. The reason is that each sovereign has an interest independent of the other in punishing the conduct. To permit one sovereign to frustrate the interest of the other by initiating prosecution first would unacceptably deprive the other sovereign of its right to enforce its own laws.

Example: A police officer is prosecuted for assault in state court for using excessive force to arrest. He is acquitted, and is then prosecuted in federal court for violating the arrestee's civil rights in the same arrest. There is no double jeopardy violation.

B. APPLICATIONS

1. **Reprosecution after an acquittal.**
Reprosecution after an acquittal is always barred. Any disposition on the merits, however styled, constitutes an acquittal, *e.g.*, not guilty verdict, directed verdict of acquittal, appellate reversal on grounds of insufficiency of the evidence. Trial and lower appellate court rulings unrelated to guilt or innocence do not constitute an acquittal.

2. **Reprosecution after a mistrial.**

a. **Mistrial with defendant's consent.**

1) Reprosecution generally permissible

2) Exception: if judge or prosecutor intended to provoke mistrial motion

b. **Mistrial over defendant's objection.**
Reprosecution permissible if there was "manifest necessity" for mistrial (e.g. hung jury, obvious procedural error in trial).

3. **After appeal.**

a. **By defendant:** reprosecution after successful appeal by defendant is permissible, unless the appeals court finds the trial evidence insufficient to sustain the (now overturned) guilty verdict.

b. **By prosecution:**

1) The prosecution cannot appeal trial rulings after acquittal because a retrial would violate the double jeopardy clause.

2) Prosecution may appeal pre-trial rulings before trial takes place or sentence decisions after the trial, where permitted by statute.

4. **Collateral estoppel.**

a. If defendant's acquittal necessarily involved a jury finding that the prosecution failed to prove a particular fact beyond a reasonable doubt, double jeopardy bars prosecution attempts to prove that fact in another criminal prosecution ***(Ashe v. Swenson)***.

b. Collateral estoppel does not apply against the defendant, only against the prosecution.

c. Collateral estoppel does not apply in a proceeding in which a lower standard of proof is used (e.g. sentencing, forfeiture proceeding, other acts evidence).

5. **Raising double jeopardy before trial.** Although procedures differ among jurisdictions, double jeopardy is usually raised and resolved prior to trial on the merits. Fed. R. Crim. Proc. 12.

a. **Questions of fact.** In many jurisdictions, if the claim of former jeopardy raises a question of fact, it is submitted to the jury along with guilt-innocence issues. In federal courts, there is no right for a jury determination of the facts, and the determination of the merits of a claim of former jeopardy is made by the trial judge.

b. **Interlocutory appeal.** The denial of a double jeopardy claim is a final, appealable order. This is so because the double jeopardy clause protects against not only double punishments, but also repeated trials.

VIII. PRETRIAL RIGHTS AND PROCEDURE

A. PROBABLE CAUSE TO DETAIN AND ADVICE ON COUNSEL RIGHTS

1. **Initial review.** A defendant is entitled to a probable cause determination by a neutral and detached magistrate as to the need to impose any restrictions on his liberty. Therefore, a defendant, who is not arrested on the basis of a warrant and not yet indicted by a grand jury must be presented to a magistrate for a probable cause determination concerning continued restraint of the arrestee within 48 hours of the arrest. This finding may be made on the face of an affidavit.

2. **Presumption of regularity.** There is a rebuttable presumption of regularity if the initial appearance occurs within 48 hours and a rebuttable presumption of irregularity if the initial appearance takes place outside of 48 hours.

3. **Remedy for violating the 48-hour rule.** The Supreme Court has not yet fashioned any remedy, such as an exclusion of evidence, for violations of the 48-hour requirement.

B. BAIL AND PRETRIAL DETENTION

1. **Preference for release on recognizance.** Modern state constitutions mandate a preference for release on the defendant's own recognizance, except for capital cases.

2. **Bail cannot be used to punish.** In any case, bail cannot be used as punishment. The function of bail is limited to the purpose of assuring the presence of the defendant at subsequent court appearances.

3. **Bail eligibility factors.**

   a. Nature and circumstances of the offense charged,

   b. Weight of the evidence against defendant,

   c. Financial ability of the defendant to post bail, and,

   d. Character of the defendant.

4. **Denial of bail.** Bail may be denied where the defendant presents a flight risk or a threat to the community. The Eighth Amendment states that "Excessive bail shall

not be required." However, the Court has not yet held that the Eighth Amendment provision pertaining to bail applies to the states. Thus, the best Constitutional argument opposing an alleged arbitrary denial of bail is due process. All detainees must be given a chance to establish eligibility for release under applicable state law.

C. GRAND JURY

1. **Indictment by grand jury before being bound over for trial on a felony charge is not constitutionally required.** As with the Eighth Amendment bail provision, the Fifth Amendment requirement of indictment by grand jury is not a right applicable to state criminal prosecutions.

2. **Information.** An alternative to indictment by grand jury is the filing of an information. An information is a written accusation of the charge prepared and presented by the prosecutor to the court, usually based on a finding of probable cause at a preliminary hearing. Charge by information is primarily practiced by some states West of the Mississippi.

3. **Role of grand jury.** Grand juries have two distinct functions:

    a. **Check on overzealous prosecution (shield).** The primary function is to conduct an independent review of the prosecution's evidence and the underlying basis for the charge.

    b. **Investigate crimes (sword).** A separate function is to investigate and detect possible crimes.

4. **Defendant's rights at grand jury.** The judiciary's role is primarily limited to the issuance and enforcement of subpoenas. No trial rights attach at grand jury proceedings. Given extensive and explicit statutory rules of criminal procedure governing grand jury at both the federal and state level, the Supreme Court has hesitated to create substantive constitutional rights in this area.

    a. **Racial bias in selection of the grand jury.** A constitutionally valid trial corrects for most defects at the grand jury. One key exception is that an indictment by a discriminatorily selected grand jury requires *per se* reversal of the ultimate conviction. However, racial discrimination in the election of the foreman of the grand jury does not require reversal of a subsequent conviction.

    b. **Grand jury secrecy.** Because of its investigatory role and the need to conduct wide-ranging investigation without a requirement to show probable cause, grand jury proceedings are secret. Violations are punishable by the contempt power of a court.

c. **No right to presence at grand jury hearings.** The target of the grand jury has no right to be present during grand jury proceedings, nor the right even to notification that he is the target.

d. **No right to Miranda warnings at grand jury hearings.** Because the prosecutor need not notify the potential defendant that he is a target of the grand jury, it follows that the defendant does not face overt coercion and therefore he has no right to receive ***Miranda*** warnings.

e. **No right to refuse to appear or not bring requested documents.** The Fourth Amendment does not apply to subpoenas to testify. Therefore, there need be no showing of probable cause or even reasonable suspicion. Testimony and production is compelled by the contempt power of the court. The trial judge may, however, hear a challenge to unreasonable requests for production of documents or other tangible items.

f. **No right to counsel.** A witness before a grand jury has no right to counsel during her testimony nor at any other part of the proceedings. The defense has no right to exclude evidence (except that seized in violation of Title III), shield other witnesses as part of her defense, produce exculpatory witnesses, or present a defense.

g. **No evidentiary rules. A** grand jury may indict on the basis of hearsay evidence or any other evidence otherwise subject to exclusion at trial.

5. **Witness Fifth Amendment rights.** See section on the privilege against self-incrimination above.

D. JOINDER OF OFFENSES OR DEFENDANTS

There are two basic issues involving joinder of offenses or defendants. The first is whether offenses/defendants may be joined for prosecution at the same trial, and the second is whether either party can compel separation of offenses/defendants so joined.

1. **Joinder of offenses.** Fed.R.Crim.Proc. 8(a) states: Two or more offenses may be charged in the same indictment or information if the offenses charged, whether felonies or misdemeanors or both

a. are of the same or similar character, or

b. are based on the same act or transaction, or

c. on two or more acts or transactions connected together or constituting parts of a common scheme or plan.

2. **Joinder of defendants.** Fed.R.Crim.Proc 8(b) states: Two or more defendants may be charged in the same indictment or information if they

   a. are alleged to have participated in the same act or transaction, or

   b. in the same series of acts or transactions constituting an offense or offenses.

   Such defendants may be charged in one or more counts together or separately, and all of the defendants need not be charged in each count.

3. **Relief from prejudicial joinder.** Fed.R.Crim.Proc. 14 authorizes trial courts, on motion by either the prosecution or the defense or *sua sponte*, to grant relief from prejudicial joinder notwithstanding satisfaction of Fed.R.Crim.Proc. 8 (a) or (b). At its election, the court may order separate trials of counts, grant a severance of defendants, or provide whatever other relief justice requires. Prejudicial joinder of defendants may result from:

   a. defendants' antagonistic defenses,

   b. a co-defendant's Fifth Amendment refusal to give exculpatory evidence, or

   c. the introduction of one defendant's confession that incriminates another defendant.

   The *Bruton* problem. Trial of co-defendants presents a special problem where one defendant has given a confession implicating his co-defendant. If the confessor elects to assert his Fifth Amendment privilege against compelled self-incrimination at trial, the co-defendant would be denied his Sixth Amendment privilege to confront an accuser if such a confession was admitted. Thus, a defendant may be severed to avoid this possibility (e.g., McVeigh and Nichols). Other means of addressing the problem are to have one trial with two juries (e.g., Menendez brothers), or to redact the confession to ensure that if multiple actors are indicated in the confession, the identity of the co-defendant is not self-evident on the face of the confession.

E. SELECTIVE PROSECUTION

1. **Selective prosecution.** Selective prosecution consists of the allegation that the laws are enforced unevenly across differing demographic groups.

2. **Standard of review.** The requirements for a selective-prosecution claim draw on ordinary equal protection standards. Thus, the claimant must demonstrate that:

   a. the prosecutorial policy had a discriminatory effect, and

   b. that it was motivated by a discriminatory purpose.

3. **Method of proof to show discriminatory effect.** To establish racial discrimination, the claimant must show that similarly situated individuals of a different race were not prosecuted. A defendant is not entitled to discovery on a claim that the prosecuting attorney singled him out for prosecution on the basis of his race without a threshold showing that the Government declined to prosecute similarly situated suspects of other races.

   Example: A survey showing that every prosecution for crack cocaine case closed in a given year involved defendants from the same racial minority without specific evidence that similarly situated defendants from other races were not prosecuted did not meet the threshold entitling defendant to discovery as to prosecution motives.

F. DISCOVERY

1. **Generally.** Criminal defendants have no constitutional right to discovery.

2. **Prosecution's affirmative duty to disclose.** The Supreme Court has imposed an affirmative duty on the prosecutor to disclose evidence favorable to the defense in its possession, however. This duty is based on the due process clause. Key details of this duty are as follows:

   a. **Affirmative duty applies to all government agents who aid the prosecution.** This affirmative duty applies to any member of the prosecution team, including the police. Nondisclosure constitutes a violation irrespective of the good faith or bad faith of the prosecution.

   b. **Evidence relevant for sentencing as well as the merits.** The government must disclose all evidence material either to guilt or to punishment.

   c. **Impeachment.** This duty includes impeachment evidence, particularly concerning the benefits a prosecution witness will receive for testifying, especially for important prosecution witnesses. A plea bargain can validly waive the right to disclosure of favorable impeachment information.

   d. **Request is irrelevant.** Favorable evidence is material and must be disclosed, regardless of whether or not a defendant made a request.

   e. **Standard of review for constitutional error.** Constitutional error results from suppression of favorable evidence by the government, if there is a reasonable probability that, had the evidence been disclosed to the defense, the result of the proceeding would have been different. As with evaluation of actual ineffective assistance of counsel claims, the materiality of the omission need not be such as to necessitate a different trial result; rather the omission need only undermine confidence in the outcome of the trial.

3. **Defense's duty to disclose.** Most jurisdictions by statute require the defense, if it so intends, to notify the prosecution of its intent to present an alibi or insanity defense.

   a. **Alibi.** The defense and prosecution must exchange witness lists relating to the alibi defense. However, at trial the prosecution may not comment on the defendant's failure to produce a witness named as supporting the alibi. If the defense later elects not to go forward on the alibi defense, the prosecution may not comment on the failure.

   b. **Insanity.** The accused often must give notice of intention to raise an insanity defense and must submit to psychological examination by prosecution doctors.

4. **Statutory rules vs. Constitutional rules of discovery.** The statutory rules of criminal procedure governing discovery differ significantly from constitutional requirements. The difference is that the statutory rules of discovery typically impose reciprocal duties of disclosure on the defense whereas the constitutional rules do not.

G. SPEEDY TRIAL

1. **The Sixth Amendment guarantees the right to a speedy trial.** This right has been incorporated by the Fourteenth Amendment and made binding on the states. The Constitution right has no rigid standards and therefore tends largely to be eclipsed by statutory rules of criminal procedure, which set specific time limits, specific triggers, and specific time suspension events. For example the Federal Speedy Trial Rule provides for a 70-day clock for defendants held in pretrial confinement and a 90-day clock for all others. However, the Constitutional rule is a backdrop to statutory rules, and notwithstanding compliance with the applicable statutory rules, a speedy trial motion should also include a Constitutional claim.

2. **Triggering the speedy trial clock.** The Constitutional speedy trial requirement is triggered by either arrest or confinement.

3. **Standard for evaluating prejudicial delay.** A Constitutional denial of a speedy trial claim is evaluated on a four-factor test. These factors are:

   a. length of the delay,

   b. reason for the delay,

   c. defendant's responsibility to assert his right, and

   d. prejudice to the defendant.

H. COMPETENCY TO STAND TRIAL

1. **Due process right.** The conviction of an incompetent defendant, or the failure to provide an adequate competency determination, violates the due process right to a fair trial.

2. **Competency and insanity distinguished.**

   a. **Insanity.** The insanity defense is a defense to a criminal charge based on the defendant's mental condition at the time he committed the charged crime. A defendant acquitted by reason of insanity may not be retried and convicted, although he may be hospitalized under some circumstances.

   b. **Competency.** In contrast, incompetency to stand trial is not a defense to the charge, but rather is a bar to trial. It is based on the defendant's mental condition at the time of trial. If defendant later regains his competency, he can then be tried and convicted.

3. **Standard.** A defendant is incompetent to stand trial if he either

   a. lacks a rational as well as factual understanding of the charges and proceedings, or

   b. lacks sufficient present ability to consult with his lawyer with a reasonable degree of understanding.

   c. The state may place on the defendant the burden of proving by a preponderance of the evidence, but requiring the defendant to show by "clear and convincing" evidence is unconstitutional.

I. PRETRIAL PUBLICITY

1. **The Sixth Amendment guarantee of impartial jurors.** Publicity, either before or after the trial, can prejudice jurors to the extent that it violates a defendant's right to an impartial jury under the Sixth Amendment. Jurors need not be totally ignorant of the facts and issues involved. Juror exposure to information about a defendant's prior convictions or to news accounts of the crime with which he is charged does not alone presumptively deprive the defendant of due process as long as the juror is "equal to the task" of impartial judgment. Venire persons may be rehabilitated on voir dire by affirming that they will be fair despite what they have heard.

2. **Standard.** To establish juror partiality, the defendant must show that publicity either prejudiced an individual juror or so pervaded the trial as to raise a presumption of inherent prejudice.

3. **Remedy.** The remedy for excessive pretrial publicity prejudicial to the defendant is a change of venue or retrial in rare cases.

J. CONFRONTATION AND COMPULSORY PROCESS

1. **Confrontation.** The Sixth Amendment provides a criminal accused with the right to confront the witnesses against him. This right has effects on three different aspects of a criminal trial.

   a. **Witness testimony in presence of defendant.** Generally, the defendant has a right to be physically present while a witness testifies against him (face-to-face confrontation). This right may yield when:

      1) defendant is voluntarily absent from the courtroom or continually disruptive after warnings from the court.

      2) if, in the case of a child witness, the presence of the defendant causes such trauma that the particular witness could not communicate.

   b. **Right of cross-examination.** The defendant has a Sixth Amendment right to cross-examine adverse witnesses. This includes cross-examination on the witness' factual knowledge and credibility, especially possible bias. Undue restriction on cross-examination thus can rise to the level of a Sixth Amendment violation.

   c. **Confrontation and hearsay.** Out-of-court statements offered against the defendant may violate the defendant's right of confrontation, regardless of whether those statements are admissible under the hearsay/evidence rules. The Confrontation Clause only pertains to the use of "testimonial" statements, not "non-testimonial" statements:

      1) A statement is "testimonial" when the statement is given under "circumstances objectively indicat[ing] . . . that the primary purpose of the interrogation is to establish or prove past events potentially relevant to later criminal prosecution." Most statements given during police interviews gathering information about past events will be considered "testimonial." In addition, drug lab reports used to prove a substance is an illegal drug is a "testimonial" statement.

      2) A statement is "non-testimonial" when "made in the course of police interrogation under circumstances objectively indicating that the primary purpose of the interrogation is to enable police assistance to meet an ongoing emergency." Other types of statements that do not meet the definition of "testimonial" may also be considered "non-testimonial," such as business records or statements in furtherance of a conspiracy.

Example: Statements given during a 911 call reporting events as they happen, as part of a request for emergency assistance, are "non-testimonial." Statements given to police after they arrive at the scene, describing what just happened, are "testimonial."

d. **Admissibility of testimonial and non-testimonial statements.** If an out-of-court statement is "non-testimonial," then the Confrontation Clause does not apply and its admissibility depends on the rules of evidence (such as hearsay). If an out-of-court statement is "testimonial," then it cannot be admitted against the defendant unless:

1) The witness who gave the statement is unavailable; ***and***

2) The defendant had a prior opportunity to cross-examine the witness.

2. **Compulsory process.** The Compulsory Process Clause gives the defendant the right to offer the testimony of favorable witnesses and to compel their attendance at trial.

a. the testimony must be material and favorable to the defendant.

b. procedural rules may not arbitrarily limit the defendant's ability to present favorable testimony (e.g., accomplice testimony, hypnotically refreshed testimony).

IX. ADJUDICATION

A. GUILTY PLEAS

1. **Plea negotiations.** The defendant may plead guilty, not guilty, or *nolo contendre.*

a. Statements made during plea negotiations in which a prosecutor was present which did not result in a plea agreement are not admissible at trial.

b. However, as a condition to entering into plea negotiations, the prosecutor is permitted to seek defendant's agreement to waive the plea-negotiation statement exclusionary provisions, and absent some affirmative indication that the defendant entered the agreement unknowingly or involuntarily, such agreements are valid and enforceable

2. **Requirements of a guilty plea agreement/waiver analysis.** A guilty plea is a waiver of Sixth Amendment rights to a trial, confrontation, subpoena witnesses, and jury, and to the Fifth Amendment right against compelled self-incrimination, and as such requires the prosecution to show that the relinquishment of the Constitutional rights in question is: 1) knowing, 2) intelligent, and 3) voluntary.

Moreover, the judge must ensure there is a factual basis for the plea. This requirement is met by a hearing addressing each of these factors (and governed by Fed.R.Crim.Proc. 11).

a. **Knowing.** Knowledge is established by showing that the trial judge specifically informed the defendant of the offenses charged, any defenses obvious from the nature of the charges, and the sentencing consequences of the plea, as well as trial rights being surrendered. Collateral consequences of conviction need not be told to the defendant.

b. **Intelligent.** The trial judge must establish that the defendant understands the consequences of the plea.

c. **Voluntariness.** Voluntariness is established by the trial judge's inquiry as to the existence of a plea bargain and any promises made to the defendant. There can be no hidden or *sub rosa* agreements or understandings. Voluntariness is not undercut merely because the defendant must choose the lesser of two evils. As long as the options before the defendant are legitimate consequences of his predicament, the election of a lesser evil is voluntary.

d. **Factual basis.** Rule 11 (F.R.Crim.P.) requires that the court assure there is a factual basis for the guilty plea. If the defendant enters a guilty plea while asserting his innocence, the court may accept the plea, but only if there is strong evidence of guilt (***Alford*** plea).

3. **Timing and withdrawal.** F.R.Crim.P. 32(d) provides that on motion before sentencing is imposed or imposition of sentence is suspended, the court may permit withdrawal of the plea upon a showing by the defendant of any "fair and just reason." At any later time, a plea may be set aside only to correct a miscarriage of justice.

4. **Later attack.** A conviction resting upon a plea of guilty or *nolo contendre* can be attacked in several ways.

a. **Failure to satisfy waiver rules (embodied in F.R.Crim.Proc. R.11).** The defendant can seek appellate relief on the ground that the plea was not accepted in compliance with the applicable procedures.

b. **Coerced.** Despite compliance with F.R.Crim.Proc.R 11, courts may permit a collateral attack on the grounds that the plea was coerced.

c. **Jurisdictional defects.** A guilty plea does not waive jurisdictional defects such as failure of indictment to state an offense, subject matter jurisdiction, or an indictment that on its face violates double jeopardy.

d. **Breach of plea agreement by prosecution.** If the prosecution breaches a plea agreement, the court may allow withdrawal of the plea, may alter the sentence, or may order specific performance.

5. **Appeal.** In most states, a guilty plea waives all non-jurisdictional errors occurring at or before trial. A conditional guilty plea, where accepted by the court, allows the defendant to appeal specified pretrial rulings, usually on motions to suppress.

B. IMPARTIAL JUDGE AND JURY

1. **Judge.** Impartial judges and juries are trial rights guaranteed by the Sixth Amendment. Judges are usually selected by a random process, but may withdraw if they are related to any of the parties at trial or stand to profit financially from relationships with any of the parties at trial. Judges can also be recused on the basis of an appearance of impropriety. Judges may also be removed for cause, but judicial bias is scrutinized on a extremely high standard and is not reviewable.

2. **Jury Trial**

a. **Right**

1. **Constitutional:** if authorized penalty exceeds six months (nonpetty cases).

2. **Waiver:** in nonpetty cases, defendant automatically receives a jury unless defendant makes a voluntary and knowing waiver.

b. **Voir Dire:** trial judge alone or trial judge and counsel for both sides can examine prospective jurors under oath. Trial judge acting alone must allow state and defense to supplement with additional questions.

c. **Size**

1. **Felony:** 12 jurors

2. **Misdemeanor:** 8 jurors

d. **Challenges**

1. **For cause:** substance addict; insufficient knowledge of English; relationship with defendant, counsel, or witness; prior or present connection to the case, actual bias; refusal to consider death penalty in capital cases.

2. Peremptory:

a. May be exercised for any reason, except race, ethnicity, or gender (violation of jurors' equal protection rights).

b. Exercised alternatively starting with prosecutor.

c. In capital cases each side has 6 peremptory challenges; in other felonies 4; in misdemeanor cases 3.

Printed in Dunstable, United Kingdom

91218881R00038